First World War
and Army of Occupation
War Diary
France, Belgium and Germany

20 DIVISION
Divisional Troops
Divisional Salvage Company
7 August 1915 - 31 March 1916

WO95/2110/4

The Naval & Military Press Ltd
www.nmarchive.com
Published in association with The National Archives

Published by

The Naval & Military Press Ltd

Unit 10 Ridgewood Industrial Park,

Uckfield, East Sussex,

TN22 5QE England

Tel: +44 (0) 1825 749494

www.naval-military-press.com

www.nmarchive.com

This diary has been reprinted in facsimile from the original. Any imperfections are inevitably reproduced and the quality may fall short of modern type and cartographic standards.

© Crown Copyright
Images reproduced by permission of The National Archives, London, England, 2015.

Contents

Document type	Place/Title	Date From	Date To
Heading	2110/4		
Heading	20th Division 20th Divl Salvage Coy. Aug 1915-Mar 1916		
Heading	20th Divl. Salvage Coy. Vol 1		
Heading	War Diary Of Capt. A.J.B. Weare, XIth To (Service) Batt Durham Light Infantry Officer Commanding XXth Divisional Salvage Company, B.E.F. France. From 6th August To 31st December 1915 Volume 1		
War Diary	Merris	07/08/1915	30/08/1915
War Diary	Neauveau Monde	31/08/1915	24/11/1915
War Diary	Sailly	25/11/1915	31/12/1915
Heading	20th Divl.-Salvage Infantry Vol 2		
Heading	War Diary Of Capt. A.J.B. Weare XIth (Service) Batt. Durham Light Infantry Officer Commanding XXth Divisional Salvage Company B.E.F. Volume 2 From 1st To 31st January 1916		
War Diary	Sailly-Sur La-Lys.	01/01/1916	12/01/1916
War Diary	Blaringham	12/01/1916	22/01/1916
War Diary	Oxelaere	23/01/1916	31/01/1916
Heading	20th Salvage Coys Vol. 3		
War Diary	War Diary Of Capt. A.J.B Weare XIth (Service) Batt. Durham Light Infantry Officer Commanding XXth Divisional Salvage Company B.E.F. Volume 3 From 1st To 29th February 1916		
War Diary	Oxelaere	01/02/1916	03/02/1916
War Diary	Esquelbecq	04/02/1916	09/02/1916
War Diary	Elverdinghe Camp	10/02/1916	29/02/1916
Heading	20 Div Salvage Coy Vol 4		
Miscellaneous	War Diary Of Capt A.G.B. Weare XIth Service Batt Durham Light Infantry (Pioneer) Officer Commanding XXth Divisional Salvage Coy B.E.F. Volume IV		
War Diary	H.Q. Camp Elverdinghe Rd.	01/03/1916	31/03/1916

20TH DIVISION

20TH DIVL SALVAGE COY.
AUG 1915 - MAR 1916

20th Brit: Salvage Coy:
vol: I

121/7909

Aug 15
mar 16

CONFIDENTIAL.

WAR DIARY

OF

Capt. A. J. B. WEARE,
XIth (SERVICE) BATN DURHAM LIGHT INFANTRY.

OFFICER COMMANDING,
XXth DIVISIONAL SALVAGE COMPANY,
B.E.F. FRANCE.

FROM 6TH AUGUST TO 31ST DECEMBER 1915.

VOLUME I.

ORIGINAL

Army Form C. 2118

WAR DIARY
or
INTELLIGENCE SUMMARY.
(Erase heading not required.)

Instructions regarding War Diaries and Intelligence Summaries are contained in F. S. Regs., Part II. and the Staff Manual respectively. Title pages will be prepared in manuscript.

Place	Date	Hour	Summary of Events and Information	Remarks and references to Appendices
Mersin	August 7/8/15		IX.th Divisional Salvage Company formed with 1 Officer, 1 Sergeant and 46 O.R.	
	8.th		Arranged Details of Company and formed nucleus of 4 Sections.	
	9.th		Visited Divisional Areas and acquainted myself with all Billets in same.	
	10.th		Further detail of 1 Sgt. and 23 O.R. joined. Sgt. Eldridge, Senior Sergt.	
	11.th		Provided Fatigue Party of 10 men to 51st Sanitary Section. 6 men to A.P.M. for Police duties. Billet Company in Evered Mounting.	
	12.th		Provided Fatigue parties as on the 11th Aug.	
	13.th		Provided Fatigue party of 1 NCO 70 men to Mobile Vet. Section. Usual drill.	
	14.th		Provided Sanitary and Police Fatigues.	
	15.th		No Remark.	
	16.		Visited 59th Brigade Area with 2 Sections and cleared & cleaned Billets recently occupied.	
	17.th		Continued work of 16th Aug.	
	18.th		Found Divisional H.Q. Guard of 1 Sgt. and 30 O.R.	
	19.th		Same as 18th (Still finding Guard).	
	20		Completed clearing 59th Brigade Area.	

Army Form C. 2118.

WAR DIARY
or
INTELLIGENCE SUMMARY.
(Erase heading not required.)

Instructions regarding War Diaries and Intelligence Summaries are contained in F. S. Regs., Part II. and the Staff Manual respectively. Title pages will be prepared in manuscript.

Place	Date	Hour	Summary of Events and Information	Remarks and references to Appendices
Merris	August 21st		Visited 60th Brigade area and viewed Billets. Divine Service.	
	22nd			
	23rd		Visited 61st Brigade area and cleared Billets.	
	24th		Provided Fatigues for Sanitary Section and Mobile Refining Section	
	25th		Again visited 61st Brigade Area and completed clearing same.	
	26th		Visited 60th Brigade Area started clearing same	
	27th		Finished 60th Brigade Area. Visited 91st Artillery Brigade and Ammunition Col. Found Dist. N. 2. Guard.	
	28th		Cleared Dist H.Q. Area after division had moved, also visited 92nd Brigade R.F.A. Went to Estaires to find new Billets. Area 3 days return in advance.	
	29th		Visited 93rd Brigade R.F.A. and Ammunition Col.	
	30th		Company moved to new Area at Nouveau Monde.	
	31st		Visited all Billets in and around Laventie. 59 to 61st Bns	
Nouveau Monde	September 1st		Found Fatigue of 6 men as Cyclists to Divl. Signal Company, this is to	

T2134. Wt. W708—776. 500000. 4/15. Sir J. C. & S.

WAR DIARY
or
INTELLIGENCE SUMMARY.

(Erase heading not required.)

Army Form C. 2118

Place	Date	Hour	Summary of Events and Information	Remarks and references to Appendices
Hameau Morelle	Sept. 1st		A steady fatigue. Drilled Coy in fire control.	
	2nd		Provided men as orderly to Recreation Room, Estaires, permanently.	
	3rd		Provided Arm't H.Q. Guard. 30 men.	
	4th		No remarks. Weather fine.	
	5th		Visited Billets of 3rd Brigade R.F.A. and cleared same.	
	6th		" " " 61st Inf. Brigade and cleared same.	
	7th		Provided fatigue of 4 men to Camp Commandant (Permanent)	
	8th		Visited and cleaned & cleared Billets of 66th Brigade who were temporarily in our Area. Fatigue of 20 men to A.D.M.S.	
	9th		Visited Billets in Estaires, Laventie. Found Arm't H.Q. Guard 30 men.	
	10th		Provided drinking fatigue to visit Laventie.	
	11th		" " for A.D.M.S. Handed A.J.S.C. collected stores.	
	12th		Found Arm't H.Q. Guard 30 men. Visited Laventie Fort and buried 5 dead bodies killed by shell fire and demolished a house that had been invaded by shell fire, (under orders of the Battery Commander). Received my orders from A.A. & Q.M.G.	

Army Form C. 2118

WAR DIARY
or
INTELLIGENCE SUMMARY.
(Erase heading not required.)

Instructions regarding War Diaries and Intelligence Summaries are contained in F. S. Regs., Part II. and the Staff Manual respectively. Title pages will be prepared in manuscript.

Place	Date	Hour	Summary of Events and Information	Remarks and references to Appendices
Hernicourt Hurdle	Sept 13th		Visited Parents and received Situations, then visited Billets been Road End and collected some S.A.A. Biscuits, Bully Beef. Cleaned out but place generally in order.	
	14th		Company changed Billets to opposite side of road. Endeavoured to arrange hire of horses, did not succeed.	
	15th		Provided fatigue to A.D.M.S. for Sanitation Purposes. Company was medically inspected.	
	16th		Provided Guard at First A.D. H.Q. fatigue of 12 men to A.D.M.S.	
	17th		Visited Billets in Return and Cleaned same. Company provided with numerous fatigues for A.D.M.S. Again failed to hire horses transport. So that Rum also refused some difficulty. Company Arms & Blankets for sick men.	
	18th		Provided First N.Z. Guard. also fatigue of 14 men to A.D.M.S.	
	19th		Provided 14 men to A.D.M.S. No other Remarks.	
	20th		do. do.	
	21st		do. do.	
	22nd		do. do. Arranged with Maire of Petainer for the Hire of Wagons and horses at the price of 6 francs per day each one.	

Army Form C. 2118

WAR DIARY
or
INTELLIGENCE SUMMARY.
(Erase heading not required.)

Instructions regarding War Diaries and Intelligence Summaries are contained in F. S. Regs., Part II. and the Staff Manual respectively. Title pages will be prepared in manuscript.

Place	Date	Hour	Summary of Events and Information	Remarks and references to Appendices
Meerut Murder	Sept. 23rd		Received Dist. H.Q. Guard, arranged that wagons do not come until the 25th. Weather fine, ordure shelling going on.	
	24		Whole Company ordered to Stand to & await orders from A.A.T.M.G. Rain commenced at evening. Intermittent shelling going on.	
	25		Tremendous Battle took place. Attack made in portion of line held by this Division by 12th Batt. Rifle Brigade. Intense Bombardment opened at 5.50 A.M. Company stand to all day. Weather very wet. Interpreter attached. 4 wagon horses were hired but not used. Received 3rd Corps orders re hiring wagons and horses, with instructions to pay for same personally through my Interpreter. Op No. 679, Divne.	
	26		Battle still goes on near trenches at the Head of Wurstwick Road. Birkage & Ducks Bill.	
	27		Visited trenches W. Esnuth Post and arranged to take all Rifles, equipment left by Casualties in them.	
	28		Visited trenches with 22 men and cleared an enormous	

Army Form C. 2118.

WAR DIARY
or
INTELLIGENCE SUMMARY.
(Erase heading not required.)

Place	Date	Hour	Summary of Events and Information	Remarks and references to Appendices
Kemmel Shrode	Sept. 28 (Cont).		Amount of Arms, Equipment & ammunition. Handed over. Ammunition Col. 96 R. Rif. SAA.	
	29th		Company still in front line trenches. Clearing same. Weather wet. Established dump at Spinette Farm at head of Trench Railway. Handed 12th Batt. Rifle Brigade Equipment to replace that lost in action.	
	30th		Visited Pont-du-Hem & conferred with Salvage Officers of newest Division about new part of line taken over by the 25th Divis. and decide the best way to work same. Company engaged in clearing Rifles and Equipments collected. Company again in front line trenches at The Bird Cage, and also Reserve trenches.	
	Oct. 1st		Company still engaged in clearing trenches and brought back 100 Bombs handed same to Bomb School orders seemed not to salve bombs. These were not collected by Salvage Coy, but were dumped in their trench by someone else.	

Army Form C. 2118.

WAR DIARY
or
INTELLIGENCE SUMMARY.
(Erase heading not required.)

Instructions regarding War Diaries and Intelligence Summaries are contained in F. S. Regs., Part II. and the Staff Manual respectively. Title pages will be prepared in manuscript.

Place	Date	Hour	Summary of Events and Information	Remarks and references to Appendices
Mauricourt Woods	3-10-15	—	Company engaged in cleaning and sorting stores salved.	
	4-10-15	—	Company provide fatigue parties.	
	5-10-15	—	Company visit trenches and billets in Rear. Various goods salved.	
	6-10-15	—	Company engaged in carting salved goods to storehouse. P.C. Charges exchanged	
	7-10-15		Visited Yorkshire Regts. Billets. Relieved some men. Charges not satisfactory. Changed for another with Mobile Vet. Section. New one satisfactory.	
	8-10-15		Visited Meaut movement Area and proceeded to clear same, getting all salved goods to railhead on the Bronfay Road.	
	9-10-15		Company engaged in carting goods from railhead to storehouse; experienced with Brigade Major of 60th Bde. as to best means of dealing with all abandoned stuff in trenches. Handed to C.S.M. Res. S.A.A. Horse wagon	
	10-10-15		Company visited Trenches Area Bird Cage, Main St. Saved all the S.A.A. in dug-outs in Lillerloy near Main St.	
	11-10-15		Company visited Trenches Sunken Road Area. Collected 2 wagon loads of goods. Handed 68 rifles to 1st Emergency dump and S.A.C. to OC R.O. OC. Big cannonade takes place.	

Army Form C. 2118

WAR DIARY
or
INTELLIGENCE SUMMARY.
(Erase heading not required.)

Instructions regarding War Diaries and Intelligence Summaries are contained in F. S. Regs., Part II. and the Staff Manual respectively. Title pages will be prepared in manuscript.

Place	Date	Hour	Summary of Events and Information	Remarks and references to Appendices
Mazingarbe	12/10/15		Medical Inspection of Company.	
	13/10/15		Company visited trenches, area Lonkur Road, Mounted George L Ky battle in our front trench, this day. Capt. Lloyd St D&L wounded. 60th Brigade area now clear, all spare ammunition stored or collected. Handed A.D.S. 366 tins Bully beef and 2 cases of Biscuits. The whole of the 63rd Bde rendered every assistance to the Salvage Coy while engaged in cleaning the area.	
	14/10/15		Handed 63rd Armourers Kirk 180 Rifles. Company on Fatigue.	
	15/10/15		Handed S.O.S. 496 tins Bully beef. " "	
	16/10/15		One Section of Coy sent to Front handed D.A.L. 63 000 Rds S.A.A.	
	17/10/15		Company still engaged on Fatigue.	
	18/10/15		do	no remark.
	19/10/15		do	do
	20/10/15		do	do
	21/10/15		do	O.C. on leave
	22/10/15		do	do

T2134. Wt. W708—776. 500000. 4/15. Sir J. C. & S.

Army Form C. 2118

WAR DIARY
or
INTELLIGENCE SUMMARY.
(Erase heading not required.)

Instructions regarding War Diaries and Intelligence Summaries are contained in F. S. Regs., Part II. and the Staff Manual respectively. Title pages will be prepared in manuscript.

Place	Date	Hour	Summary of Events and Information	Remarks and references to Appendices
Hameau Morale	23/10/15		Company on Fatigues O.C. on leave. No remarks	
do	24/10/15		do do do	
do	25/10/15		do do do	
do	26/10/15		do do do	
do	27/10/15		do do do	
do	28/10/15		do O.C. returned from leave do	
do	29/10/15		do No Remarks.	
do	30/10/15		One Section on Salvage Work in Trenches Remainder employed on fatigues	
do	31/10/15		do do	
do	1/11/15		Company Engaged in Casting Poles and Brushwood from Forest.	
do	2/11/15		do do	
do	3/11/15		do O.C. visited Rugby Post to report on same. Same bound it abandoned and reported according. Heavily shelled while there.	
do	4/11/15		Company still Engaged in Forest Fatigues. do	
do	5/11/15		do	
do	6/11/15		do	

WAR DIARY
or
INTELLIGENCE SUMMARY.
(Erase heading not required.)

Army Form C. 2118

Place	Date	Hour	Summary of Events and Information	Remarks and references to Appendices
Hazebrouck Meerut	5/11/15		Company Engaged on Fatigue Works. No remarks.	
	6/11/15		do do	
do	9/11/15		do Visited Billet of W Riding Regt in Estaires	
			Took over turned goods from them	
do	10/11/15		Provide Guard to Coal Shaft at Laventie. Usual Fatigues	
do	11/11/15		do do	
do	12/11/15		Seized various goods in Laventie do	
do	13/11/15		Usual guards and Fatigues. No remarks.	
do	14/11/15		do do	
do	15/11/15		Handed 83rd Coy. R.E. 42 Acces Picks and 84 Shovels F.S. Handed all stores in storeroom to D.A.D.O.S. for transmission to Rouen. (Lt. Jones No. 2 & 2. Coys)	
do	16/11/15		Company still engaged in handing over stores.	
do	17/11/15		do	
do	18/11/15		do	
do	19/11/15		do	
do	20/11/15		Company Engaged on Renewed Fatigues.	

Army Form C. 2118.

WAR DIARY
or
INTELLIGENCE SUMMARY.
(Erase heading not required.)

Instructions regarding War Diaries and Intelligence Summaries are contained in F. S. Regs., Part II. and the Staff Manual respectively. Title pages will be prepared in manuscript.

Place	Date	Hour	Summary of Events and Information	Remarks and references to Appendices
Lawrence Monde	21/11/15		Company Engaged on Fatigues. No Remarks.	
	22/11/15		do	
do	23/11/15		do	
do	24/11/15		Company move with Division to SAILLY-SUR-LA-LYS. Opened Theatre. C.C. Engages to look after and run the Theatre.	
SAILLY	25/11/15		Company Engaged on Fatigues	No Remarks
do	26/11/15		do	do
do	27/11/15		do	do
do	28/11/15		do	do
do	29/11/15		do	do
do	30/11/15		do	do
do	1/12/15		do	do
do	2/12/15		do	do
do	3/12/15		do	do
do	4/12/15		do	do
do	5/12/15		do	do

T2134. Wt. W708—776. 500000. 4/15. Sir J. C. & S.

Army Form C. 2118.

WAR DIARY
or
INTELLIGENCE SUMMARY.
(Erase heading not required.)

Instructions regarding War Diaries and Intelligence Summaries are contained in F. S. Regs., Part II. and the Staff Manual respectively. Title pages will be prepared in manuscript.

Place	Date	Hour	Summary of Events and Information	Remarks and references to Appendices
SAILLY	6/12/15		Company engaged on Fatigues. No Remarks.	
do	7/12/15		Company issued 16.800 Rds S.A.A. from Billets at Hendricin.	
do	8/12/15		Company on Fatigues. No Remarks.	
do	9/12/15		do	
do	10/12/15		do	
do	11/12/15		do	
do	12/12/15		do	
do	13/12/15		do (arrived recruits from 12th R.B.)	
do	14/12/15		do	
do	15/12/15		do	
do	16/12/15		do	
do	17/12/15		do	
do	18/12/15		do. Smoke Helmet drill	
do	19/12/15		do. No Remarks.	
do	20/12/15		Served on F. G. C. M. Company engaged on Fatigues. No Remarks.	

Army Form C. 2118.

WAR DIARY
or
INTELLIGENCE SUMMARY.
(Erase heading not required.)

Instructions regarding War Diaries and Intelligence Summaries are contained in F. S. Regs., Part II. and the Staff Manual respectively. Title pages will be prepared in manuscript.

Place	Date	Hour	Summary of Events and Information	Remarks and references to Appendices
SAILLY	21/12/15		Company Engaged on Fatigue	No Remark
do	22/12/15		do	do
do	23/12/15		do L.T. gave evidence at F.G.C.M. Knocked off horse by motor.	
do	24/12/15		do (Christmas Eve)	
do	25/12/15		Visited men at Dinner	
do	26/12/15		Kit Inspection	
do	27/12/15		Company on Fatigue	No remark
do	28/12/15		do	do
do	29/12/15		do	do
do	30/12/15		do	do
do	31/12/15		Prepared Gala Concert for Theatre and succeeded very well. Record takings fr.200.15	

20th Div¹ Salvage
Company
Vol: 2

Confidential

War Diary

of

Capt: A. J. B. Weave.
XI.th (Service) Batt. Durham Light Infantry.

Officer Commanding
XX.th Divisional

Salvage Company

B.E.F.

Volume 2.
From 1st to 31st January 1916.

Original

WAR DIARY
or
INTELLIGENCE SUMMARY.
(Erase heading not required.)

Army Form C. 2118.

Place	Date	Hour	Summary of Events and Information	Remarks and references to Appendices
SAILLY-SUR LA-LYS.	1st Jany 1916		Company provided fatigue for loading coal at SAILLY Station and unloading same at Batts.	
do	2nd "		Coal fatigue as on 1st Jany.	
do	3rd "		do	
do	4th "		do	
do	5th "		do	
do	6th "		do	
do	8th "		do	
do	9th "		do	
do	10th "		Cleared store houses for Brigade Stores and began to receive same	
do	11th "		Received final orders re move and arranged transport and allotted same. 3 Lorries Bt.1. 1 A/Tt Commander. 2. 2 Officers. 1 Signal Coy. 1. 96th Coy. R.E. 1. 63rd Coy. R.E. 4. Salvage Coy. Loaded and turned same ready to move at 7.0 Am on 12th	
do	12th "		Whole Company engaged in transporting forward H.Q. Stores to BLARINGHAM. Arrived BLARINGHAM at 11.0 AM.	

Army Form C. 2118.

WAR DIARY
or
INTELLIGENCE SUMMARY.
(Erase heading not required.)

Instructions regarding War Diaries and Intelligence Summaries are contained in F. S. Regs., Part II. and the Staff Manual respectively. Title pages will be prepared in manuscript.

Place	Date	Hour	Summary of Events and Information	Remarks and references to Appendices
BLARINGHAM	1916 12th Jan cont		and proceeded to post guards and coal stores. Thoroughly cleaned out Officers, Sergeants Messes House, and Billeted Men.	
do	13th		Company engaged in Coal & Ration fatigues, and also Guard over Coal, 1 N.C.O. & 4 men.	
do	14th		same as 13th	
do	15th		do	
do	16th		do	
do	17th		do	
do	18th		O.C. Coy. went on leave Coy was Commanded by 2nd Lt. Henman	
do	19th		do	
do	20th		Provided usual fatigues also 10 men to Sanitary Sec. & 20 for Coal.	
do	21st		do	
do	22nd		Coy. received orders to move to OXELAERE. The following fatigue duties were provided. 8 men for guarding Baggage at HAZEBROUCK. Provided Guards & fatigue parties at OXELAERE for Batt. H.2.	

T2134. Wt. W708—776. 500000. 4/15. Sir J. C. & S.

Army Form C. 2118.

WAR DIARY
or
INTELLIGENCE SUMMARY.
(Erase heading not required.)

Instructions regarding War Diaries and Intelligence Summaries are contained in F. S. Regs., Part II. and the Staff Manual respectively. Title pages will be prepared in manuscript.

Place	Date	Hour	Summary of Events and Information	Remarks and references to Appendices
OXELAËRE	1916 Jany 23rd		Company provided fatigue parties for cleaning Village and also found Guards over Wood and Coal Stores.	
do	24th		do	
do	25th		do	2nd Lt. Coy. Returned from Leave.
do	26th		do	
do	27th		Inspection of Company.	
do	28th		Paid Company.	
do	29th		do	
do	30th		do	
do	31st		do	

20th Salvage Coys
Vol: 3

Original

Confidential

War Diary
of
Capt: A.J.B. Neave.
XI.th (Service) Batt. Durham Light Infantry.

Officer Commanding
XX.th Divisional
Salvage Company
B.E.F.

Volume 3.

From 1st to 29th February 1916.

Army Form C. 2118.

WAR DIARY
or
INTELLIGENCE SUMMARY.
(Erase heading not required.)

Instructions regarding War Diaries and Intelligence Summaries are contained in F. S. Regs., Part II. and the Staff Manual respectively. Title pages will be prepared in manuscript.

Place	Date	Hour	Summary of Events and Information	Remarks and references to Appendices
Eecloure	31/1/16		Visited Poperinghe with A.D.D.M.S. and selected Huts to hut stores & baggage	
"	1/2/16		Proceeded from Hazebrouck to Poperinghe with 16 lorry loads & unloaded same	
"	2/2/16		Moved Company from Eecloere to Squelberg billets &c	
"	3/2/16			
Squelberg	4/2/16		Company on General Fatigue work in new billets	
"	5/2/16		Company moved from billets. Engaged in hauling wood from station.	
"	6/2/16		Sanitary fatigues in Poon.	
"	7/2/16		do	
"	8/2/16		do	
"	9/2/16		Selected 2 Coies of Horse sheds from Farm at Wormhoudt handed to D.A.D.S	
Elverdinghe Camp	10/2/16		Company ordered to move to new Headquarters. Proceeded to A.72.d.7.h.6 2.8 and Proceeded to receive R.E. in preparing new Camp.	
do	11/2/16		do	
do	12/2/16		do	
do	13/2/16 14/2/16		do	
do	15/2/16		Camp Fatigue Salvage work. Windmill Farm. 300 Rum jars. 80 Motor tyres (old) 1 ton. of 303 S.A.A. 24 Water Bottles. 50 Petrol tins empty. 10 S.S. Shovels. to D.A.D.O.S.	
do	16/2/16		Camp fatigues. Salvage work. 6 doz Bully beef. 4 Drums Grease.	

WAR DIARY
or
INTELLIGENCE SUMMARY

Army Form C. 2118.

Place	Date	Hour	Summary of Events and Information	Remarks and references to Appendices
Shorncliffe Camp	13/2/16 (cont)		3 Drums of Chloride of Lime, 1 drum Laboratory Cal. 2 Hand Numbers 63 Rifles Slings. Rifle 100 Bayonets 30. Cycles 2. Oil bottles 250 Pull Throughs 160	
	16/2/16		Sent parto 3 etc. 80 tins bully beef.	
	17/2/16		Rifles 2. 8000 Rds SAA. 1 case Ballistite.	
	18/2/16		Rifle 3. Shell Cases 10 Roses 2000 Rds SAA. 7 Tents complete (20 mans)	
	19/2/16		Rifle 1. 8000 Rds SAA quantity of equipment various (to WASTE)	
			Supplied 60 Tents w.l. with 80 Petrol Tins	
	20/2/16		5000 Rds SAA. D.A.Q.	
	22/2/16		1 Cycle. Handed to 85 Coy R.E. Various Camp fatigues	
	23/2/16		Camp fatigues. Lavatories dug out.	
	23/2/16		6 Rifles 1 Case of Bombs (handed to Trendale Offrs) 1 Revolver Stn	
			Shells, 1 fuse Detonator 1 fuse bomb fuse (handed to Bomb officer)	
	24/2/16		Camp fatigues. Building Augosts.	
	25/2/16		2 Rifles. 5 Steel Helmets. 31 pairs Gum Boots Thigh. 4 Sheep skins	
			5 Waterproof sheets. 14 Horses Very slight quantity of small arms	
	29/2/16		Company engaged in returning school goods to Railhead.	

Place	Date	Hour	Summary of Events and Information	Remarks and references to Appendices
Boulogne Rifle Camp	28/9/16		2000 Rds R.S.A 15 pair Boots Enid (Knight) 44 Rifles 1000 Rds S.A.A. Part of by Brickburg Brigade Returned to D.A.D.O.S. 13 Complete Lents expended	
	29/9/16			

2 Div Salvage
Coy

Vol 4

Original

Confidential

WAR DIARY
OF

Capt A.J.B. Weare
XI:th Service Batt. Durham Light Infantry.
(Pioneer)
Officer Commanding
XX:th Divisional Salvage Coy.
B.E.F.

VOLUME IV.

Army Form C. 2118.

WAR DIARY
or
INTELLIGENCE SUMMARY.
(Erase heading not required.)

Instructions regarding War Diaries and Intelligence Summaries are contained in F. S. Regs., Part II. and the Staff Manual respectively. Title pages will be prepared in manuscript.

Place	Date	Hour	Summary of Events and Information	Remarks and references to Appendices
H.Q. Camp Elverdinghe Rd.	1/3/16		Medical Inspection of Company. 15 Men employed digging dugouts. Company also carried large amount of Stores. Salvage work and digging fatigue	
do	2/3/16		do	
do	3/3/16		do	
do	4/3/16		do	
do	5/3/16		do	
do	6/3/16		do	
do	7/3/16		do	
do	8/3/16		do (Pionr Coy)	
do	9/3/16		do	
do	10/3/16		do	
do	11/3/16		do	
do	12/3/16		do	
do	13/3/16		do	
do	14/3/16		do	
do	15/3/16		do	

Army Form C. 2118.

WAR DIARY
or
INTELLIGENCE SUMMARY.
(Erase heading not required.)

Instructions regarding War Diaries and Intelligence Summaries are contained in F. S. Regs., Part II. and the Staff Manual respectively. Title pages will be prepared in manuscript.

Place	Date	Hour	Summary of Events and Information	Remarks and references to Appendices
H.Q Camp Sheerngha	16/3/16		Med. Inspection of Coy. Digging fatigue and salvage work	
do	17/3/16		Salvaging Area of Division Digging fatigue.	
do	18/3/16		" "	
do	19/3/16		" "	
do	20/3/16		" "	
do	21/3/16		" "	
do	22/3/16		" "	
do	23/3/16		" "	
do	24/3/16		" "	
do	25/3/16		" "	
do	26/3/16		" Pte at Coy killed.	
do	27/3/16		Barn burnt out. No Casualties. Salvaging and Area digging fatigue.	
do	28/3/16		" "	
do	29/3/16		" "	
do	30/3/16		" "	
do	31/3/16		" "	

www.ingramcontent.com/pod-product-compliance
Lightning Source LLC
Chambersburg PA
CBHW081249170426
43191CB00037B/2089